What Cannot Stay Small Forever

poems by

Sean Webb

Finishing Line Press
Georgetown, Kentucky

What Cannot Stay Small Forever

Copyright © 2019 by Sean Webb
ISBN 978-1-64662-100-2 First Edition
All rights reserved under International and Pan-American Copyright Conventions. No part of this book may be reproduced in any manner whatsoever without written permission from the publisher, except in the case of brief quotations embodied in critical articles and reviews.

ACKNOWLEDGMENTS

"In the Wings" first appeared in different form in the chapbook *The Constant Parades*
"Playground" first appeared in *Schuylkill Valley Journal*

The title of this collection comes from the last line of Heather McHugh's poem "The Size of Spokane"

Publisher: Leah Maines
Editor: Christen Kincaid
Cover Art and Author Photo: Colleen Quinn, colleenquinnart.com

Printed in the USA on acid-free paper.
Order online: www.finishinglinepress.com
　　　　　also available on amazon.com

Author inquiries and mail orders:
Finishing Line Press
P. O. Box 1626
Georgetown, Kentucky 40324
U. S. A.

Table of Contents

In the Wings 1

Admittance 2

Playground 3

My Horse 4

First Currency 5

Behind Hedges 6

Heaven 7

While a Distant War Raged On 8

The Pose 9

Chute 10

Bread Bags 11

A Dream of Flight 12

Doing Time at a Christian Kindergarten 13

Sewer Pond 15

Terrible Creature 16

The War in Geiger Heights 17

This Dungeon Was almost an Empire 18

Genesis 19

Starting Lineup 20

Returns 21

Expo 74 22

Broken Love 23

Independence Day 24

Jenny Hanivers 25

Legend 26

Boy on an Inner Tube 27

*In loving memory of my mom, Karen Webb.
And for my dad, Alan, brother Scott and Sister Michele.
Thanks for getting me through those early years.*

In the Wings

Before I was born, my mother
worked in a fish cannery in Alaska.

In the slime room she relieved
fish of their last workings, cleared

corners of entrails for market.
I was sequestered in a body

isolated in a factory, hung out
over water. I was an intense act

of labor and desperation.
A brine shrimp in the works.

Admittance

On the day I was born
the Saturday Evening Post

trumpeted *Armageddon!*
on its dusky scarlet cover.

I couldn't have known this.
Newly alive I was taken

to my grandparent's house
on the west side of Spokane.

Dad still stationed in Alaska,
Mom had three in tow now.

Pine, sagebrush, and dust
found those new receptors

that forever in my brain
associate with *home*.

Playground

My first memory—hot sand
under bare feet, wildly

painted metal horse,
dragon's fiery red tongue,

gun-metal gray monkey
bars high over head

crawling with screaming
kids lunging at rungs.

My Horse

Suddenly
I see my horse

on coiled springs,
jockey children

reeling wildly
lurching into

and out of
control.

First Currency

Plucked from a beach—
unearthly sand dollars.

Coarse ivory skin.
Incalculable worth.

Each displayed a star
on the sky of itself

resting in the universe
of my outspread hands.

Behind Hedges

The villages I created elated me.
I paved roads with playing cards,

placed trees where I believed
they belonged, and buildings

made of small boxes. I formed
hills with tiny horizons and drove

Matchbox cars over them into
the unknown. I imagined all

the people—having nothing
I could find to stand for them

the way I thought they should
be in the world I made myself.

Heaven

No one else was on the street
after a downpour came and went.

I followed a stick on its voyage
down the river in the gutter.

I imagined tiny towns dotting
the river's edge peopled with

mothers and fathers and children
living little lives. And then

a slow boy in a yellow rain
slicker appeared from the blue

to carefully place the drowned
worms in a big red lunchbox.

While a Distant War Raged On

I was terrified using the men's room
in Shadle Park. I was five years old,

it was 1968, someone convinced me
that I would be castrated one day.

I wasn't even sure what that was.
Whether they would cut my nuts

or dick off. It was always dark
in there and seemed like a place

that could happen. I hated going
inside, waiting for it, wondering

which they'd cut off, and why.
I was five, my father was off

in a war, it was sunny and hot
and I held my mother's hand

every day when we walked to
the playground at Shadle Park.

The Pose

Why, in old photographs,
do young boys stand

with their shoes smack
against each other like

huddled rodents, hands
plastered to their sides

at attention, or startled
awareness that they must

shape up for the camera
(that will not lie)

in that moment they
look so inadequate in

and will be captured
for all days?

Chute

Mom warned me I'd be killed
if I slid down the laundry chute

into the spider-ridden basement.
After broken bones, burns, stitches

that resulted from every rule I defied,
for some reason I believed that one.

The long drop in a galvanized passage
to a basement that already seemed full

of death, surely looked terminal.
But I mulled it over every day—

creaking open the chute's door,
staring into black waiting space.

Bread Bags

My mother saved them all.
Wonder bread bags. Circles

of primary colors arranged
on milky white plastic. She

pulled them over my holey
winter boots to keep melting

snow out. When I bathed
with broken bones, one

would be pulled over
and cinched to protect

the soluble plaster casts
that provided necessary

space and time that
my bones might heal.

A Dream of Flight

Two by fours, broken halves
of a roller skate and rusty nails

from a coffee can would fulfill
the dream of flight. We didn't

have a giant log, or the where-
withal to hollow one out, or a river

to paddle away on—some dreams
remained abstractions. But this,

we could fly over the driveway
and sidewalks. It could work.

We set to sawing and hammering
the pieces together but then we

must have disagreed on something.
I beat him up and pinned his legs

over his head until he couldn't
breathe. He was my friend

I played with every day
as long as my will be done.

Doing Time at a Christian Kindergarten

I rode in a seat attached to my mother's bike
to the Christian kindergarten up the street.

I'm fond of saying they beat us mercilessly
but there was something less than mercy.

The lickings were reasoned and measured.
They (the old crones) read bible stories

about candy-coated murders and betrayals
for hours on end. Any kid who fidgeted

got taken into the next room and swatted
with a ping pong paddle—a lick added

each time they had to take you back.
The hyper kids were in the thirties.

I was bored by the whole thing—
the mother and son of each letter hung

over the blackboard, primary colors
on everything, little dunces all around me

who could not recognize their own names.
But I was rapt by the story of Lot's wife.

When we colored her, I colored her white
of course, and looked with disdain at

renderings in purple, red, and brown.
I was intrigued by the processional

of Noah's animals. But I suppose it was
to hammer home the tediousness that

they had us color an endless scroll
of giraffes, lions, elephants, doves . . .

One day a window got broken. Honestly,
I don't recall if I did it, but a kid said I did.

I also don't remember my punishment
but I remember his, meted out in the yard.

If not for intervention, I was determined
to run over the world like Caligula.

Sewer Pond

Out beyond the gravel pit, we walked
muddy banks, shooting spent rubbers

floating in shitty water, with our bb guns,
sewage bubbling up from each toilet

flush in our nearby military housing
complex. One day, some kids floated

out into the pond on air mattresses
to try to catch ducklings. We fell in

and swam to shore empty handed,
dripping foulness on flowered banks.

Terrible Creature

One day I saw on the windowsill
a hornet with its head bowed in death.

(It was late afternoon and light beams
were swarmed with swirling motes.)

I was too young then to question
whether that was an act of resignment

or simple contracture. I did wonder
if it had a soul. And why wouldn't it?

They told me I had one. And what else
would continually compel the hornet

to hover in its stripes about my face—
there being nothing there to lift

its enormous eyes to that might love it
and provide a measure of comfort.

The War in Geiger Heights

Some kids spent long days
assembling elaborate models

of tanks and planes. Others
gathered up their G.I. Joes

and plastic toy soldiers.
We took them to the woods

and blew the hell out of 'em
with m-80s and cherry bombs

and set the remains ablaze.
The G.I. Joes that survived

got random limbs torn off
and painted red with nail

polish blood. After there was
nothing left to destroy, we split

into teams and viciously hunted
each other until the streetlights

came on and we were called
to the vicissitudes of home.

This Dungeon Was Almost an Empire

I took a wrong turn somewhere
and wound up in the hands of my jailers.

The gang of four boys who I had kept
in their places, climbed a tree and waited

for me to walk home from school. Together,
they pissed from high up in the branches

on me. Something snapped. It was
as if the magnetic poles shifted

and Hyperborean giants
sank back into the sea.

Genesis

It was the *world* that we created,
in honor of Johnny Horizon, stuffing

tissues into a chicken wire globe
sitting on a trailer hitched to a tractor.

Our Lutheran youth group walked
behind it in the Junior Lilac Parade

waving at strangely excited families
that lined the curbsides for blocks.

I was mortified. I know that much.
That early bitter seed of shame

had broken through the skin
and was beginning to blossom.

Starting Lineup

Before a season of football
we stood, a line of eleven-

year-olds, pants around
our ankles. A nurse reaching

under our genitals, pressing
a place behind our sacks and

commanding us to turn heads
and cough, unavoidably on

the boy next to us. This,
and the disgrace of jam

jars sloshing with piss,
was our induction to fall.

Returns

For money, I collected cases
of fresh empties from the big

drinkers and gathered bottles
and cans from rural roadsides.

I hauled it all in an old red
wagon with no other use left.

The skunky empties—Lucky,
Rainier, Mickey's Big Mouth,

and the char of cigarette butts
doused in dregs, filled my nose.

When the garage was packed
to the rafters, it was time to haul

it all to the collection place
and get my money. Stacks

of wrinkled bills I couldn't wait
to find somewhere to spend.

Expo 74

Iran and Iraq
shared a pavilion.

The world was concerned
with the world

it was becoming apparent
we were killing.

In the afternoon,
I caught the eye

of a girl in a blue gondola
drifting across the sky.

I waved while backing up
and fell over a bench.

The fire of humiliation
welling in my face

reached her through
the leaves and branches.

Broken Love

In my newfound land
of fear and degradation—

your flawless arms
and unblemished face.

Settling in
to my pre-adolescent Elba,

I offered my love with a box
of chalky messaged hearts

that you dumped
on the sidewalk—

freed from syntax,
sugaring the earth.

Independence Day

I was just starting to feel
strangely excited about *this*—

waiting until dark for celebration
(a few years later, in the desert,

I will enhance the fireworks
with massive doses of LSD).

I must've been stunned by colors
and rocked by thudding duds

of disappointment that announced
themselves seconds after a flash

but I don't recall. I only remember
a car screeching into the parking lot

that we had just returned to after
the show, a man in tattered pants

and shirt thrown out the passenger
door while the car was still moving

fast, rolling with a thud, dead
or alive into the gutter.

Jenny Hanivers

A blueberry bagel makes me think
of soft underbellies of frogs and lips

of a little girl with a hole in her heart—
her beach towel and bag of sandwiches,

her round a.m. radio and slow clouded
brother lumped on the lake's shore.

Her blonde hair adhered to wet stones
in the cold water—and skates and rays

cut up and dried, sold to passersby
as mermaids and angels and devils.

Legend

My stories grew bigger—
I shot a chipmunk in the balls

as it ran under me while I stood
on a woodpile. I shot a grosbeak

right through the eye, and came up
against a badger running through

the woods while a fire raged all
around us. I got a butt-full of rock

salt from an angry farmer, back
when there were no questions

what you could do on your land.
I don't know what's true. I shrank

and couldn't handle being smaller
than a BB, so small I could slip

out the window like a breath of
smoke. I had to puff myself up.

I wasn't enough. In this world
I never was going to be enough.

Boy on an Inner Tube

I have not been
completely honest. Perhaps

I will never be. I am no longer
the small body that once

slipped through rounded
rubber walls into seamless

black water, with only
an inflation stem scratching

my side to remind me
that I was not without fault.

Sean Webb was born in Spokane and spent his younger years in Washington, where these poems are set. He eventually moved with his family to Arizona and later lived in Iowa, New Mexico, Utah, and Pennsylvania. Over the years he worked as a paperboy, grocery bagger, dishwasher, lifeguard, waterbed maker, cook, headshop clerk, arts center house attendant, janitor, zoning enforcement tech, standardized patient, mall Santa, factory worker, meat packer, unsuccessful baby picture salesmen, and many other jobs before working as a medical writer and editor at various universities, research facilities, and publishing houses. He has three daughters and two grandsons and currently lives in Philadelphia with his wife, the artist Colleen Quinn, where he works as the managing editor and chief lexicographer of a medical dictionary.

He is a graduate of the Iowa Writers Workshop and has received many honors for his work, including fellowships from The Arizona Commission on the Arts and the Utah Arts Council. In 2005 he was selected by Grace Paley to serve as Poet Laureate of Montgomery County, Pennsylvania. Most recently he was awarded the *Passages North* Neutrino prize and was winner of the *Gemini Magazine* 2017 Poetry Open. His chapbook *The Constant Parades* was selected by Afaa Weaver as a runner-up in the 2017 Moonstone Poetry chapbook competition. His work has appeared in many publications including *Prairie Schooner, North American Review, Greensboro Review, Nimrod, The Quarterly, The Seattle Review, Schuylkill Valley Journal,* and *West Branch*. Additional information about the author and links to other poems can be found at *seanwebbpoetry.com.*

www.ingramcontent.com/pod-product-compliance
Lightning Source LLC
LaVergne TN
LVHW041514070426
835507LV00012B/1570